BEFORE YOU BUY ANOTHER POLICY

Poonam Guptaa
Business Insurance Strategist

Available on amazonkindle
Worldwide Published by
Pendown Press
PREMIUM BUSINESS PUBLISHER

PENDOWN PRESS LLP
An ISO 9001 & ISO 14001 Certified Co.,
Regd. Office: 3767A, Kanhaiya Nagar,
Tri Nagar, Delhi-110035
Ph.: 8130886000, 9650072927
E-mail: info@pendownpress.com
Branch Office: 1A/2A, 20, Hari Sadan, Ansari Road,
Daryaganj, New Delhi-110002
Ph.: 011-45794768
Website: PendownPress.com

Edition: 2025
Price: ₹299
ISBN: 978-93-6338-831-4

Layout and Cover Designed by Pendown Graphics Team
Printed and Bound in India by Thomson Press India Ltd.

To everyone who ever felt lost in the world of money and insurance.
May this book be your guide.
And to my daughters (my strength), this is for you.

Table of Contents

PREFACE

Sometimes, the most important things in life are the ones we understand the least.

For many people, insurance is one of them.

This book isn't written to show how much I know. It's written because I've seen how many people don't know, and how costly that lack of knowledge can be.

Over the years, I've met people who paid their premiums faithfully, only to have their claims rejected. People who signed forms without reading, trusted blindly, and thought insurance was just paperwork. I've seen families struggle not because they didn't care, but because no one told them what really matters while buying a policy.

And all this made me ask myself:

Why don't we talk about insurance the way we talk about saving, earning, or even buying a phone?

This book is a small effort to bring that missing conversation into your hands. I've tried to write it in the simplest words I can. No big terms. No expert talk. Just straight from the heart.

This is not a textbook. It's a conversation. From my heart to yours: **Simple, Clear,** and **Honest**.

If you've picked up this book, thank you. It means you care about your future, your family, or maybe even just understanding things better.

And if by the end of it, you feel a little more confident, a little more prepared that's more than enough for me.

Let's begin this journey with honesty and clarity.

Poonam Guptaa
Business Insurance Strategist

□ □ □

ACKNOWLEDGEMENTS

To my universe my Krsna: thank you for aligning the right people, right moments, and right lessons at every turn.

To my mentor, Akshar Yadav Ji: your kind words stayed with me through the tough days. You made me believe that my story matters.

To my husband, Dhirendra Gupta: your calm and steady support has been my anchor. You stood beside me, even when my dreams were just quiet thoughts. Your faith in me spoke louder than any fear I had.

To my daughters, Deepti, Deepika & Megha: thank you for your lovc, your patience, and your understanding when I couldn't always be there. You all are my biggest reason to keep going

Neeraj and Sumeet: thank you for always encouraging me to move forward. Your belief in me has been a silent strength, empowering me to move forward to become a bigger person in life.

To my grandchildren, Ananya, Aarav and Agastya: thank you for motivating me by calling me your Role Model. That one line meant the world to me and inspires me to do better every day.

To my parents and in-laws: your trust and blessings have always given me strength. You laid the base that helped me walk this path.

To my amazing team and Aansh: this book has my name, but your efforts, ideas, and energy are in every chapter. Thank you for believing in the message of Before You Buy Another Policy and walking this journey with me.

To Mr. Dinesh Verma and the entire Pendown Press team: this book wouldn't exist without your commitment, creativity, and care. Thank you for bringing it to life.

And lastly, to every friend, family member and well-wisher whether named or unnamed, your presence in my life is a blessing.

This book holds a part of me, but it also holds a part of each one of you.

□ □ □

Know Your Author

Poonam Guptaa

Founder - Insure 360° | Financial Educator | 45+ Years of Impact

From nurturing young minds in classrooms to transforming financial journeys across continents, **Poonam Guptaa's story is one of purpose, reinvention, and service.**

After a celebrated **21-year career as a Principal**— where she was **honoured with awards like Best Principal by CBSE**— Poonam stepped into the world of finance not for business, but for people. The shift wasn't planned; it was inspired.

This new journey began with a simple yet powerful question someone asked her:

"If you care so much about people being misguided in insurance, why don't you do something about it?"

That one question changed everything.

It gave birth to **Insure 360°**—a financial advisory that doesn't focus on selling policies but on solving real problems, spreading awareness, and earning trust.

Now, with over 45 years of professional experience, thousands of happy families, and global recognition across 5+ continents, Poonam Guptaa stands as a veteran advisor and ethical voice in India's insurance industry.

Her mission has remained unchanged since day one—

- Never sell a product, until you understand the person.

- Never push for a plan, without first understanding their pain.

Every client at Insure 360° is guided with care, personalised strategies, and the goal of building not just wealth—but peace of mind.

She now leads this mission alongside her two daughters and a dedicated team of experts, turning what began as a one-woman vision into a growing force for ethical advisory and client-first service.

This book is her honest and heartfelt attempt to demystify insurance, expose common traps, and share the financial secrets India's wealthiest already use—from **tax-saving techniques to building generational wealth through smart planning.**

Because she believes:

- When people are informed, they are empowered.
- And when money is protected, dreams are possible.

(Poonam Guptaa)

(Megha Gupta)

(Deepika Gupta)

❑ ❑ ❑

Why This Book?

1. **Because insurance was never meant to confuse you.**

   This book clears the clutter—with real stories and honest advice.

2. **Because one wrong decision can cost your family everything.**

   And the right guidance can protect generations.

3. **Because you've been sold policies—never truly explained them.**

   It's time someone sat with you, like family, and made it make sense.

4. **Because you shouldn't wait for a claim to realise a mistake.**

   This book helps you get it right—before it's too late.

5. **Because no one else told you the truth.**

   But now, you'll know what the wealthy already do.

6. **Because financial peace comes from preparation—not luck.**

   And your peace of mind is worth planning for.

7. **Because it's not just about returns—it's about responsibilities.**

   The right policy can protect your dreams, not just your money.

□ □ □

INTRODUCTION:
BEFORE YOU DOUBT INSURANCE—READ THIS FIRST

In today's world, the word "investment" has become almost synonymous with excitement.

Crypto coins promising 200% returns, startup pitches that sound like the next unicorn, IPOs that fly on day one—it's thrilling.

Amid all this, insurance can feel boring.

Safe.

Slow.

Outdated.

But here's the truth no trending reel or Twitter thread will tell you:

Insurance isn't supposed to excite you. It's supposed to protect you.

And that, my friend, is its biggest strength.

Let's take a step back.

Before we begin our 9 powerful lessons, let's address the elephant in the room:

Why Do We Still Need Insurance in a Crypto-Obsessed World?

Because financial success is not just about returns. It's about resilience.

When life throws its worst at you—a health emergency, a business loss, a sudden accident—it's not your crypto wallet or stock portfolio that steps in.

It's your insurance. When the world shakes, insurance holds firm.

What Insurance Offers That Volatile Assets Don't

- **Protection from Catastrophic Losses**
  - Hospitalisation, surgeries, loss of income, legal liabilities—insurance shields your savings when things go wrong. It's not just a policy. It's your safety net.
- **Stability & Predictability**
  - Insurance-linked savings plans, annuities, and retirement products offer guaranteed or steady returns. Not flashy, but reliable and sometimes, that's exactly what you need.
- **Tax Benefits**
  - Sections like 80C and 10(10D) provide tax advantages that most high-risk investments don't. Insurance helps you save smarter while you grow.
- **Peace of Mind**
  - With insurance in place, you don't stay up at night thinking "what if something happens tomorrow?" Instead, you sleep better because you're protected.

Still Think Insurance Is a Poor Investment?

Imagine this:

You invest ₹20 lakh in crypto.

You invest ₹20 lakh in a retirement insurance plan.

One may give you a wild return.

The other will give you a guaranteed future, tax benefits, and emotional peace.

There's no wrong choice—just incomplete ones, if made without understanding.

The richest people in the world don't choose between risk and safety.

They balance both.

And that's exactly what I want you to do, too.

My Final Word Before We Begin

This book isn't about promoting one product over another.

It's about helping you ask the right questions.

Insurance is a tool.

If you understand it, use it wisely, and align it with your goals—it can build and protect generational wealth.

So before you buy another policy, or worse—ignore it altogether—read on.

The best lessons are just a few pages away.

□ □ □

Lesson

01

The Illusion of Convenience

Why Online Insurance Might Cost You More Than You Think

In today's digital-first world, buying insurance online seems like the fastest, smartest option. A few clicks, a shiny policy PDF in your inbox, and you're "covered."

But here's what no one tells you:

When it's time to claim, you're often alone.

- No advisor to call
- No help understanding the fine print
- No personal guidance during emergencies

And when a claim is delayed or rejected on technical grounds, who do you turn to? A toll-free number? A chatbot? Your peace of mind deserves more than that.

The Harsh Reality:

- Many online policies are designed to sell, not to serve.
- Minor documentation gaps can lead to **denied claims.**
- In times of crisis, **you need a human,** not a helpline.

What You Should Look For Instead:

- An insurance advisor who knows your needs and stands by you.
- Someone who ensures your documentation is complete, accurate and claim-ready.
- A professional who works for you, not an algorithm.

Insurance is not just about comparing premiums or ticking boxes.

It's about having someone who shows up when it matters most.

That's the difference between buying online and buying wisely.

Case Study

When Online Insurance Failed — A Real-Life Rescue

Meet **Rahul** and **Surbhi,** a young couple excited about their much-awaited trip to Europe. The tickets were booked, the itinerary was set, and their online travel insurance—through a well-known provider—seemed to be enough. Or so they thought.

But life had other plans.

- In Switzerland, Anmol met with a sudden accident.
- Panic set in. Hospitals were involved. Urgent medical attention was needed.
- They called their **online insurance support team**—and waited.
- 12+ hours passed. No solution. No assistance. Only scripted replies and frustrating delays.

What Changed Everything:

Back in India, a worried family member reached out to me.

Even though they hadn't purchased the policy through **Insure 360°**, I stepped in.

Within 24 hours:

- I coordinated directly with the insurance company
- Activated the cashless facility for immediate treatment
- Ensured a seamless payout of $50,000 towards medical bills

The Lesson?

Buying online gives you a policy.

Having an advisor gives you protection.

When you work with someone who understands both the paperwork and the people, your policy becomes a promise—not just a piece of paper.

□ □ □

Lesson

02

Don't Let a Bank Decide Your Financial Future

We often trust institutions we consider "safe"—banks, relationship managers, or long-time advisors—without questioning their motives. But when it comes to your hard-earned money, blind trust can be a costly mistake.

Many people fall into the trap of buying investment products or insurance plans suggested by banks simply because someone they know or trust recommended them. But here's what you need to know:

The Truth Behind the Desk:

- Bank RMs work on monthly targets—not your life goals.
- Their priority is commission, not your family's future.
- They are salespeople, not long-term planners.

What You Deserve Instead:

- A dedicated expert who studies your life stage, financial goals, and risk appetite.

- Customised strategies that align with your aspirations—not sales targets.
- Transparent advice that prioritises protection and wealth creation.

When you allow someone else to make decisions about your money without understanding your story, you risk turning your savings into someone else's success metric.

Always ask: Am I investing for me, or am I being sold something for someone else's bonus?

And remember: Just because a product is offered by a trusted name doesn't make it the right choice. Financial planning is not one-size-fits-all. What worked for your colleague, friend, or even your banker might be completely wrong for you. True financial advice feels like someone is walking beside you—not pushing from behind. Always choose wisdom over convenience.

Case Study

A Costly Mistake With a Hard Lesson

Ajay and Aarti, a well-settled couple from Dubai, believed they were on the right track with their investments. Like many NRIs, they trusted their bank's relationship manager (RM) back in India—assuming he would handle their money with the same care they did.

Over a span of 5–6 years, their RM repeatedly advised them to break existing investments and reinvest into new plans. Each time, the pitch was promising. The paperwork looked polished. But behind the scenes, these frequent switches benefited only one party—the RM working toward his own quarterly targets.

What Jay and Kiran didn't realize was this:

Every reinvestment came with losses—exit charges, surrender penalties, and missed compounding.

By the time they understood what was happening, their cumulative losses had ballooned to **nearly ₹1 crore**. And at the age of 65, what was supposed to be a peaceful financial phase turned into a **burden of anxiety, regret, and health issues** they never saw coming.

The Lesson

- Don't let trust replace strategy.
- Banks don't know your future dreams—**they know their sales quotas.**

- A qualified financial advisor creates a **vision-driven** plan, not a product-driven pitch.
- Long-term wealth is built with **clarity, patience,** and the **right hands guiding you.**

Jay & Kiran's story is not uncommon. But it doesn't have to be yours.

Before you invest another rupee, ask yourself—who is this investment really benefiting?

□ □ □

Lesson

03

The Small Legal Clause That Could Save Your Family's Future

When we buy life insurance, our intention is clear: we want to protect our family in our absence.

But what if—despite paying premiums for years and securing a high-value term plan—the insurance payout never reaches your wife or children?

This isn't a rare technical glitch. It's a real problem caused by one **missed step**: not attaching your life insurance policy to the **Married Women's Property Act (MWPA), 1874.**

Here's what MWPA does:

- Ensures the life insurance proceeds **go solely to your wife and/or children**—no one else.
- Legally protects the money from **creditors, banks, and courts**—even if you have debts or loans at the time of your death.
- Creates a **trust-like protection**, so that even family disputes or business liabilities can't affect the payout.

- Once attached, the policy becomes **untouchable—even by you**. You can't change the beneficiaries or surrender it without their consent.

It's one of the strongest and most underutilized tools in insurance planning.

And yet, most advisors skip this clause simply because clients never ask for it—and few understand its power.

Before you buy another policy... ask your advisor: "Have we attached MWPA?"

Because no amount of coverage is useful if it doesn't reach the ones it was meant for.

A few extra minutes spent on paperwork today can mean **unshakable protection** for your loved ones tomorrow.

Case Study

A Tragedy That Could Have Been Prevented

A close family friend's husband, a well-to-do businessman, took a term insurance policy from a bank representative. He trusted that the insurance would take care of his family if anything went wrong.

Sadly, just two years later, he passed away due to a sudden brain fever.

The insurer honored the claim and released the entire payout. But what followed shocked the grieving family.

Because the policy was not secured under MWPA, the **entire insurance amount was seized by creditors** due to settling outstanding business loans. His wife and two young children, whom the policy was meant to protect were left with nothing.

No safety net.

No financial support.

Only heartbreak, legal battles, and deep regret.

The Takeaway

If that policy had MWPA applied, **not a single rupee could have been taken by creditors.** The payout would have gone **directly and exclusively** to his wife and children.

MWPA turns an insurance policy from a financial product into a **protected family asset**

It's especially critical for:

- Business owners
- Self-employed professionals
- Anyone with loans or liabilities

Don't just insure your life—**secure your family's claim to it.**

□ □ □

Lesson

04

Health First. Life Next. Then Retirement

When people think of financial planning, they often rush to build wealth without building protection.

But here's the truth:

Your wealth means nothing if it's not protected.

The foundation of a strong financial plan isn't just about earning or investing. It's about securing what you already have and who you love, first.

An ideal insurance strategy follows a simple, yet powerful sequence:

1. ***Secure Your Health First***
   - With rising medical costs and unpredictable illnesses, **a robust health insurance plan is non-negotiable.** It protects your savings from being wiped out in a single hospital visit.
2. ***Then, Safeguard Your Life***
   - A **term insurance plan** ensures that your loved ones are not financially devastated in your absence.

3. ***Finally, Plan for Your Retirement***

    - Use **ULIPs, pension plans, or guaranteed return instruments** to build a corpus that gives you peace of mind and freedom in your golden years.

Most people reverse this order. They start with retirement or wealth creation, while ignoring risks that could derail everything. The result?

Financial stress. Uncovered risks. Poor or unstable returns.

Before You Buy Another Policy...

Ask yourself:

- Do I have adequate **health coverage** for my family and myself?
- Will my family be **financially protected** if I'm not around tomorrow?
- Have I **started early** enough to build a strong retirement fund?

A great financial future isn't built only by earning more—**it's built by protecting what you've earned.**

Case Study

Transforming Insurance into a Financial Growth Engine

Girdhari Gupta, MD of Yash Appliances, had always viewed insurance as a mere formality, just something to check off the list.

That was until he met us at **Insure 360°.**

Together, we restructured his entire portfolio with one clear goal: **Protection first, then progress.**

- Health Insurance to tackle unexpected medical expenses
- High-value Term Plan to secure his family's future
- Tailored Retirement Plan with guaranteed returns

Today, his insurance policies are **not just protection tools**—they're active contributors to his financial growth.

With **over 30 policies managed over a 17-year association,** he often says:

"She never sold me insurance. She gave me solutions."

The Takeaway

- Prioritise coverage in the right order
- Build a strategy that supports both your life and lifestyle
- Choose advisors who care about your future, not just your premiums

□ □ □

"Do not save what is left after spending; instead spend what is left after saving."

~ Warren Buffett

Lesson

05

Simplify Your Finances with a Demat Insurance Account

Let's face it—most people today have multiple insurance policies:

- Health
- Life
- Retirement
- Critical illness
- Accidents, and more...

Now imagine trying to track all of that across paper documents, email folders, agent calls, WhatsApp chats, and calendar reminders.

Sounds exhausting, right?

That's where a **Demat Insurance Account** comes in—a secure digital locker for all your insurance and investment documents, accessible anytime with just a few taps.

Why It Matters:

- **Centralised Management:** View all policies in one place
- **Timely Renewals:** Avoid missing due dates or policy lapses
- **Easy Nomination Updates:** No paperwork hassle
- **Quick Claims & Access:** Your family won't struggle in an emergency
- **Peace of Mind:** Know everything is organised, safe, and secure

Before You Buy Another Policy...

Ask yourself:

- Do I know where all my insurance documents are?
- Can my family access them quickly if needed?
- Is there a simple way to manage and track it all?

If not, it's time to consolidate. Because a well-managed portfolio isn't just smart... it's **stress-free.**

Case Study

Turning Chaos into Clarity

An established professional with high-value policies across life, health, ULIPs, and pension plans approached me with one problem—**everything was scattered.**

He had missed two premium due dates, misplaced policy bonds, and most worryingly, his family had no idea where to find things in case of an emergency.

We opened a **Demat Insurance Account,** and within days:

- All policies were uploaded and synced
- Nominations details were updated and verified
- Reminders were automated
- Every important document became accessible via a single digital dashboard

Today, he feels in control of his finances like never before.

And more importantly, **his family feels secure.**

The Takeaway

- Financial clarity is just as important as financial planning
- Simplifying systems reduces stress and saves money
- A Demat Insurance Account is not a luxury—it's a necessity

"Clutter is not just the stuff on your floor—it's anything that stands between you and the life you want to be living."

~ Peter Walsh

Lesson

06

Insure Your Business, Not Just Yourself

When we talk about insurance, most people only think of personal protection. But if you run a business—small or large—your company needs a safety net just as much as you do.

Imagine if your business suddenly lost a key partner, founder or director.

Would it survive the shock?

The harsh truth is:

Leadership changes due to illness, accident, or sudden demise can cripple a business overnight.

Without proper planning, it becomes difficult to:

- Keep operations running smoothly
- Maintain client confidence
- Fulfill financial and legal obligations

That's where **business insurance** steps in—not as an expense, but as a smart investment in stability.

Here's What You Can Do:

- **Keyman Insurance:** Covers the financial loss that can arise from losing a key employee, founder, or partner whose absence could disrupt operations.
- **Partnership Insurance:** Helps surviving partners buy out the deceased partner's shares without disturbing working capital.
- **Loan Protection:** Covers outstanding business liabilities in case of unforeseen events.
- **Business Continuity Planning:** Structured insurance ensures cash flow stability even in times of crisis.

Before You Buy Another Policy...

Ask yourself:

- Can my business survive without me or a key partner for a few months?
- Would my team, clients, or family struggle financially if something happens to one of us?
- Have I built a financial cushion for unexpected leadership or ownership changes?

If the answer to any of these is "No" or "Not Sure," then your business needs a plan—**starting now.**

Case Study

Creating a Shield for Business Stability

A client running a large infrastructure company approached us to structure their business insurance. Until then, their insurance policies were focused only on physical assets—machinery, vehicles, and premises. But nothing protected the business from **people's risk.**

We helped them:

- Identify key decision-makers
- Assess financial impact of losing one
- Implement Keyman & Partnership insurance
- Create a continuity fund via corporate insurance tools

Within a few months, the entire leadership team had structured financial safety nets.

Now, even if life throws a curveball, **the business doesn't suffer.**

The Takeaway

- Your business deserves protection too
- Key people are just as valuable as physical assets
- Insurance is not just a safety net—it's a survival and succession plan

□ □ □

"The best investment you can make is in yourself—and your business."

~ Warren Buffett

Lesson

07

Don't Let Fire or Theft Burn Through Your Finances

You took the smart step of insuring your shop, office, or factory against fire and burglary.

But here's a harsh truth that most realise only **after the damage is done:**

× Having a policy is not enough.

✓ Being prepared is what gets your claim approved.

Every year, countless business owners are left stranded—not because they didn't buy insurance—but because they couldn't provide the right documents, proofs, or updates during the claims process.

Here's What You Must Do to Protect Your Business:

1. Maintain Updated Valuation Reports

Your stock, machinery, furniture, and infrastructure must reflect **accurate and current market values.**

An outdated valuation can lead to a lower claim settlement—or even denial—on the grounds of underinsurance.

2. Keep Digital & Physical Copies of All Policy Documents

Make sure that your insurance policy, payment receipts, endorsements, and add-on covers are stored **in multiple formats**—PDFs on the cloud, printed copies in-office, and shared with a trusted family member or senior staff.

3. Prepare a "Claims File" in Advance

Don't wait for an emergency. Create a ready folder with:

- Photographs/videos of assets
- Invoices and purchase bills
- Stock/inventory records
- Asset registers or equipment logs

This ensures you don't scramble when an assessor visits.

4. Inform Your Insurer About Any Major Changes

Have you recently renovated your property?

Increased your stock levels during peak season?

Bought new machines or changed storage layouts?

Every such change must be informed to your insurer in writing.

Failure to disclose these can lead to claim rejections under non-disclosure clauses.

5. Train Your Team on Emergency Response

Make sure your staff knows where documents are stored, who to call, and how to access backups.

In your absence, your claim must still proceed smoothly.

Why This Matters:

A claim is not just a refund—it's your business's survival plan.

When disaster strikes, your ability to bounce back depends not just on the policy you bought, but on the **proof you have.**

Insurance isn't just about premium payments.

It's about preparedness.

Before you relax thinking you're covered, ask yourself:

"If something happens today... will I be able to prove my loss tomorrow?"

Case Study

A Costly Fire—And an Even Costlier Mistake

A well-established manufacturing business faced a tragic fire due to an electrical short circuit.

The damage?

Machines, raw materials, and finished goods—worth several crores—gone overnight.

When the claim was filed, the insurer requested basic documents:

valuation reports, updated stock registers, purchase invoices, and policy endorsements.

None were readily available.

What followed was a **six-month delay,** endless back-and-forth, and only a partial claim settlement due to missing data.

The result?

Cash flow was disrupted, orders were cancelled, and the business took nearly a year to recover.

Before You Buy Another Policy...

Ask yourself:

- If something goes wrong tomorrow, do I have everything ready to support my insurance claim?
- Will my family or staff know how to access the documents?

If the answer is "no," then you don't just need insurance—you need insurance readiness.

The Takeaway

- Insurance is your parachute.
- But without the right documentation, it won't open when you need it most.

Protect your wealth not just with a premium—but with preparation.

□ □ □

"Money is a terrible master but an excellent servant."

~ P.T. Barnum

Lesson

08

NRI Insurance—Global Presence, Indian Assurance

When it comes to securing your family's future, **geography should never be a limitation.**

Whether you live in Toronto, Dubai, or Sydney—if your roots trace back to India, Indian insurance policies can offer you far more than you think.

But most NRIs don't know this.

Who is Considered an NRI in Insurance?

In the eyes of insurance providers in India, you're treated as an **NRI (Non-Resident Indian)** if:

- You **reside outside India** for **more than 182 days** in a financial year
- You hold an **Indian passport** or have Indian citizenship

Others related categories include:

- **PIO (Person of Indian Origin):** Children or grandchildren of Indian citizens, typically holding an **OCI (Overseas Citizen of India)** card

- **Foreign Nationals:** Even if not of Indian origin, anyone residing in India on a valid work visa is eligible to purchase life insurance from Indian insurers, with or without an OCI card

Why Should NRIs Consider Insurance in India?

Because India's insurance landscape offers **powerful advantages** that are often overlooked:

- **GST Benefit**

  NRIs can save on taxes applicable under GST, making their insurance investments more efficient.

- **Medical Facilities in 57+ Countries**

  Top insurance plans offer international health coverage, so you're protected even while living abroad.

- **Protection + Investment**

  These policies serve dual purposes: Life cover and long-term investment—perfect for NRI legacy planning.

Why This Matters

Being away from home doesn't mean you can't **plan for it.**

Your insurance strategy should align with:

- Your current global lifestyle
- Your financial responsibilities in India
- Your desire to build and pass on wealth with confidence

In my journey, I've helped NRIs from **over 10 countries**, with access to tools supporting clients in **147 nations**. Many believed Indian insurance had no relevance to them—until they discovered its **returns, flexibility, legal strength,** and **planning power.**

Key Takeaways

✓ You don't need to live in India to insure in India

✓ You can save taxes, get global health coverage, and grow wealth in INR

✓ Most importantly, your family back home remains protected, no matter where you are

If you're an NRI—or have loved ones living abroad—this is your sign.

Explore how Indian insurance can support **global financial goals with local wisdom.**

□ □ □

"The best way to secure your child's future is not just love and education—but a strong financial foundation."

~ Poonam Guptaa

Lesson

09

Insurance for Kids – A Gift of Protection and Purpose

We all want to give our children the best of everything. But in the journey of providing love, care, and education, many parents overlook one of the most powerful tools of legacy—Insurance with Intention.

Here's a common mistake:

Many parents buy insurance in the child's name, thinking they're investing for the child's future.

But here's a truth very few will tell you—

When you insure a child, you are protecting the life of the child, not your family's future.

And in unfortunate situations where a child is affected, no amount of money can truly heal that pain. The payout becomes irrelevant.

So what should you do instead?

- **Parents should always be the proposer and the insured:** If anything happens to a parent, the payout becomes a survival fund for the child—covering education, home, support, and more.

- **Use the maturity benefit to empower your child's future:** When the child grows up, the returns from the policy can be used as their share in starting a business, investing in a home, or even pursuing a dream abroad. It's a financial gift that arrives exactly when needed.
- **Attach riders like Waiver of Premium:** This ensures if the parent is no longer around, the policy continues without any further premiums, and the child still receives the maturity benefit as planned.

Takeaway:

Buy insurance for your children, not on your children.

A small premium today can become a powerful asset tomorrow—an investment in dreams, dignity, and stability.

□ □ □

ASK BEFORE YOU ACT – THE 10 DO'S & DON'TS OF BUYING INSURANCE

In an age where everyone is selling something, insurance is no different. But unlike a gadget or a holiday package, this isn't a purchase you can afford to regret later. When you buy insurance, you're making a promise—to your future, your family, and your peace of mind.

So before you commit, ask the right questions. Here are my **Top 10 Do's and Don'ts,** learned over **45+ years of experience,** designed to help you avoid the most common—and most costly—mistakes.

Top 5 DO's Before Buying Insurance

1. **Know Your Purpose Clearly**
   - Are you buying for protection, retirement, or investment? Start with a clear goal in mind. A confused buyer often ends up with the wrong plan.
2. **Check the Company's Claim Settlement Ratio**
   - A CSR above 95% is a mark of trust. If they can't settle when needed, it's not worth buying.
3. **Read Beyond the Brochure**
   - Understand exclusions, conditions, waiting periods, and terms. Never assume—verify everything.

4. **Calculate the Right Sum Assured**
   - 10–15x your annual income is the minimum for life cover. For health insurance, adjust regularly to beat medical inflation.
5. **Consult an Experienced Financial Advisor**
   - Algorithms don't understand emotions. People do. Go beyond what's trending—seek advice based on experience, not popularity.

Top 5 DON'Ts Before Buying Insurance

1. **Don't Chase Tax Benefits Alone**
   - Yes, deductions are great—but don't lose sight of the bigger picture: financial security.
2. **Don't Buy Under Pressure—From Banks, Friends, or Family**
   - You're buying for your future. Choose the right product, not just the familiar face or voice.
3. **Don't Withhold Medical or Financial Information**
   - Be 100% honest during disclosure. What you hide now might haunt your family later.
4. **Don't Delay Insurance Until Illness or Retirement**
   - The earlier you buy, the lower the premium—and the stronger your cover. Health doesn't send a reminder before leaving.
5. **Don't Rely on Toll-Free Numbers or Apps Alone**
   - When it's time to claim, you'll wish for a human expert. Invest in relationships, not just policies.

Final Lesson:

Insurance is not just a safety net. It's a financial strategy.

It's your **plan B** when life doesn't go as planned. It's your tool to convert uncertainty into confidence, and risk into opportunity. But this only works when you treat it with the seriousness it deserves.

Before You Close This Book...

Remember:

- Don't just buy a policy. **Build a plan.**
- Don't just listen to agents. **Ask the right questions.**
- Don't delay. **The right time to act is now.**

If this book has given you even one insight that saves your money, protects your family, or helps you plan better—I've done my job.

I'm **Poonam Guptaa,** and for over four decades, **I've helped individuals, families, business owners, and NRIs take better control of their financial future.**

Now, it's your turn.

Go ahead—read smart, plan strong, and insure wisely.

□ □ □

"The investor of today does not profit from yesterday's growth."

~ Warren Buffett

The Truth Test – Why Hiding Health Conditions Can Cost You Everything

Imagine this:

You pay your premiums regularly.

You assume your family is financially secure.

But when you need your insurance the most—your claim gets denied.

Why?

Because you didn't disclose a past health condition during the application.

The Silent Risk Most People Ignore

One of the biggest and most common mistakes I've seen over the years is this:

People don't reveal their complete health history when buying insurance.

Some feel it's "too minor."

Some worry about premium hikes.

Some think—"What's the harm if I'm fine now?"

But here's the reality:

Today's insurance companies use AI-backed medical underwriting systems.

These smart algorithms can fetch historical data from:

- Past hospitalisations
- Diagnostic lab reports
- Prescription history
- Health check-up records
- And sometimes even pharmacy purchases

So, what you don't disclose—they may still find out.

And when they do, especially at the time of claim—it's flagged as non-disclosure, and your entire claim can be rejected.

A Costly Oversight, A Preventable Mistake

What people don't realise is:

Insurance isn't just about paying premiums—it's about creating trust and transparency between you and the insurer.

By hiding pre-existing conditions, even unintentionally, you risk:

- Claim denial during a medical emergency
- Wasted years of premium payments
- Leaving your family financially vulnerable when they need help the most

What Should You Do Instead?

Here's what I advise every client:

- Disclose everything—even if it feels irrelevant
- Let the insurer decide what matters medically

- Choose a trusted advisor who guides you through medical declarations
- Opt for policies with proper underwriting, not shortcuts Ask your advisor to get written confirmation of accepted conditions

Real Advice, Not Fear

I've helped clients successfully claim on policies where medical conditions were disclosed properly—because the insurance company had clarity from Day One.

It's not about hiding—it's about planning honestly and smartly.

Takeaway:

Honesty at the start saves heartbreak at the end.

□ □ □

Case Study

When Hidden History Becomes a Blocked Claim

The Situation

A client once approached me to buy a new health insurance policy for his father.

He sounded clear and confident — his only concern was getting coverage for an upcoming **knee replacement surgery.**

After understanding the case, I assured him,

"Yes, this surgery will be covered under the policy—provided there's no past record of the same condition."

But what he didn't tell me... the system revealed.

Once the insurance was issued, and the surgery date approached, the hospital's medical team conducted a routine review.

That's when the truth came out:

- His father had **already undergone two knee replacements**—one in **2012** and another in **2015**.

This prior history was never disclosed in the proposal form.

The Outcome

As per policy terms, the insurance company treated this as **misrepresentation of facts**.

The **claim was rejected**, and the client was left shocked, angry, and financially strained.

But here's the truth:

He wasn't just angry at the insurer—

He was frustrated with himself for not telling me everything in the beginning.

The Lesson

Insurance is not a guessing game.

It's a **contract based on trust.**

When you hide your medical history—even unintentionally—you're not protecting yourself... you're **risking everything.**

Your advisor isn't just a policy seller.

They're your guide who can help you navigate even the toughest conditions, **if you tell them the full truth.**

- ✓ Always disclose **everything**—even that small surgery from years ago
- ✓ Let your advisor design a plan that works **within the rules**, not outside them
- ✓ Remember: Hiding now can cost you later

Smart Investments Start with Smart Conversations

Thank you for taking the time to read this book. Your time is valuable, and I'm truly grateful that you chose to invest it here.

If any part of this book sparked a thought, raised a question, or left you wanting to go deeper—I'd love to hear from you.

Whether you have feedback, a query, or simply want to continue the conversation about building a secure financial future for your children, I'm just one message away.

Email me at: poonamgupta.n21@gmail.com

Want a one-to-one conversation? Let's schedule a quick meeting and explore how I can support your journey.

Your next step could be the one that secures a lifetime of impact.

Looking forward to connecting,

Poonam Guptaa

☐ ☐ ☐

AWARDS

Our awards aren't just achievements; they're acknowledgments of the trust we've earned, the values we uphold, and the impact we've made over the years in the insurance industry.

At **Insure 360°,** each recognition stands as a reflection of our long-standing commitment to transparency, innovation and client-first service. These awards are not just markers of past achievements; they're the catalyst that drives us to keep pushing forward with honesty, hard work, and unwavering dedication.

Dubai

Amsterdam

Greece

Georgia

Phuket

Bali

South Africa

South Korea

Pattaya

Thailand

London

HEAR IT FROM THEM

Discover real stories of confidence and security from our clients who have transformed their financial futures with INSURE 360°.

From health insurance to long-term investment planning for my entire family—kids, grandkids, and even through our business—Poonam Guptaa has handled it all with unmatched expertise. Her guidance on Employer-Employee Investment Plans has secured both our personal and business finances."

~ Mr. Surender Garg, MD, Hansa Metalics Ltd.

Poonam Guptaa has been our trusted advisor for years. From life insurance to business protection, she has seamlessly managed the complete insurance portfolio for me and my entire family. Her ability to foresee risks, simplify choices and stand by us at every step has made all the difference."

~ Mr. Amit Bansal, MD, Theon Pharmaceuticals

"Our collaboration with Poonam Guptaa has been truly transformational. Over the years, what started as a professional relationship has evolved into a personal bond—she has always been there whenever I needed support. With over 30 policies, I can confidently say she has never 'sold' us insurance—she has only ever provided solutions that work for us. Her expertise, diligent follow-ups, and ethical approach have given us complete confidence in her. More than policies, she has helped secure our financial well-being while ensuring excellent returns on our investments."

~ Girdhari Gupta, MD – Yash Appliances

MDs, Homeland Park Mohali & AB Paper Mills

"Despite being deeply involved in real estate investments ourselves, when it came to securing the financial future of our grandchildren, we turned to Poonam ji. Her expertise, clarity, and trustworthy approach gave us the confidence to make meaningful long-term investments. We're grateful for her guidance and highly value the relationship we've built with her over the years."

~ Mr. Bir Bhan Goyal & Mrs. Sunita Goyal

"Associated with Poonam ji since 1985, I proudly call her the financial Guru of my children, Sahil and Ginny. Her integrity, follow-through, and unwavering commitment set her apart. I've trusted her with my family's future—right down to investments for my grandchildren—and I confidently recommend her guidance to all who seek honest financial advice."

~ CA T.N. Singla Ji

□ □ □

Connect On LinkedIn

Visit our Website

www.insure360.in

Follow for More Updates

@insure_360